MUSTN'T DO IT!

(WAT NIET MAG...)

Jo M Van IJssel de Schepper Becker

translated from the Dutch by Laurence Senelick

BROADWAY PLAY PUBLISHING INC
224 E 62nd St, NY, NY 10065
www.broadwayplaypub.com
info@broadwayplaypub.com

MUSTNT DO IT!

First printing: September 2010
I S B N: 978-0-88145-421-5

Book design: Marie Donovan
Typographic controls: Adobe InDesign
Typeface: Palatino
Printed and bound in the U S A

CHARACTERS & SETTING

THE FATHER, *Gerard*
THE MOTHER, *Marie*
THE SON, *Walter*
THE DAUGHTER, *Lisa*
THE DAUGHTER'S FIANCÉ, *Charles*

The play is set in a provincial town in the Netherlands in the early 1920s.

The action takes place in an ordinary room of a well-to-do middle-class home.

ACT ONE

(FATHER, MOTHER *and* SON *are sitting at the table.* FATHER *is reading a newspaper,* MOTHER *and* SON *are each reading a book. The piano is open, with sheet music on it.*)

FATHER: (*Folding up the paper*) Well, there's not much news in the paper.

MOTHER: (*Absently*) Is that so?

FATHER: (*Rises and paces back and forth; to* MOTHER) Are you still planning to go out this afternoon?

MOTHER: (*Without looking up*) Me? No, dear.

FATHER: Nasty weather—you're right to stay indoors. Since I don't have to, I won't go out either. —What about you, Walt?

SON: What did you say?

FATHER: (*Mimicking good-naturedly*) What did you say? Bookworm! Play us a tune!

SON: Oh no.

FATHER: (*Sits down again, leafs through the paper, is clearly bored*) The Bolsheviks have been at it again! Have you two read about this?

MOTHER: (*Good-naturedly, but not interested*) Goodness! How awful!

FATHER: A nice little mess over in Russia! While *we're* sitting here in a bed of roses.

MOTHER: (*Laughing*) What do you want us to say, we're reading.

SON: Let us read in peace for once.

FATHER: Read in peace for once! That's all you ever do! Play the piano or read! When it comes to conversation, forget it!

MOTHER: Now, father! Live and let live.

FATHER: (*Grumbling*) You call that living? Where is Lisa?

MOTHER: With Charles.

FATHER: Charles was here—and went away without saying hello? That fellow must not like us much.

MOTHER: That occurred to *me* too. At first it was only natural that he'd come to see Lisa; but now that they're engaged, he almost never drops by.

FATHER: And then without much enthusiasm!

MOTHER: I wouldn't say that. And besides Lisa is never home. It's always: I'm going to Charles's house, or I'm meeting Charles somewhere, or Charles is going to pick me up, so I promised to be ready. —It might be more sociable if they both visited here for a change.

FATHER: Then ask them, for a change.

MOTHER: He's always so evasive. His mother is on her own, or else he's expecting a phone-call from the office...

FATHER: It's possible...

MOTHER: Yes, but it's always the same thing. It never used to be so hard for him to come by, he never used to have a problem dropping in...

FATHER: Strange... (*To* SON) Does it make any sense to *you*?

SON: (*Nervous, curt*) *Me?* No.

MOTHER: Well, you could help. Or is that too much for you?

SON: Too much for me? What's that supposed to mean?

FATHER: Walter isn't unfriendly to him.

SON: What are you getting at? There's nothing going on.

MOTHER: I get the impression that Charles is avoiding you.

SON: (*Forced laughter*) You're imagining things!

MOTHER: Well, I may be wrong.

SON: What are you reading?

MOTHER: The book about Beethoven you thought was so beautiful.

SON: Good grief, you're reading that? How do you like it?

MOTHER: (*Hesitating*) Well, I can't figure out what you think is so good about it.

SON: (*Enthusiastic*) You really can't? It's wonderful. As soon as I read it, mother, I understood his music so much better. The awful life that Beethoven led, why, he led a miserable existence. —And the section (*Takes the book*) from this page to this one, didn't you find it gripping?

MOTHER: (*As before*) Yes...yes I did...I'll read it again.

SON: Tomorrow I'll play for you what he was composing at that time...and then you'll hear...you'll feel what he was going through...

MOTHER: Yes, dear. That'll be nice.

FATHER: (*Having watched his wife in amusement, good-naturedly*) You're going to get just as highbrow as the boy. What are you doing with a Beethoven book! A chimp reading the Bible!

SON: Just because you can't see anything in it! Nobody else can enjoy it!

FATHER: Go ahead and enjoy it. There's no accounting for taste. The things I enjoy are very different.

SON: (*Mildly contemptuous*) Very!

MOTHER: (*Warning*) Walt!

FATHER: (*Bitterly*) He thinks his stupid Dad doesn't know any better.

MOTHER: (*Soothing*) There, there. —You certainly don't think that, do you?

FATHER: What a bunch of couch potatoes we have here! What do you say we three play a game of cards?

SON: Oh Jesus, cards!

MOTHER: Oh, if I know you, Walt, you'll do it to please your father.

SON: All right, go ahead then.

FATHER: Is it such a sacrifice for you? I don't get it. There's nothing wrong with a little diversion.

MOTHER: Yes—but he doesn't care for it.

FATHER: Does the kid have to waste all his free time reading and playing the piano? All right, I know he's good at it. Go on, play us something. But something entertaining; not a funeral march.

SON: (*Not at once*) I don't know anything entertaining.

FATHER: It's beneath the gentleman's dignity! Wherever I go these days I hear lively dance tunes, stuff like that; and I have to have a son who can play piano, does it a treat, and damned if I ever get to hear anything upbeat. Nothing but that highbrow music, I'm surprised you don't get sick of it!

SON: (*Coolly*) I don't get sick of it.

FATHER: Neither does your mother. She didn't always swim in such a highfalutin atmosphere.

MOTHER: What's more wonderful than to share your children's lives?

FATHER: Oh really, share their lives! We all live all together, don't we? But you used to live differently from what you do nowadays.

MOTHER: I did indeed, dear. It's through the children that I began to take an interest in art and... and the human soul, which is what creates art. Isn't that right... Walt?

SON: Yes, of course. If mother had only had more education! Because she really is like us.

FATHER: Like us? What do you mean by that?

SON: Like Lisa and I. How can I put it? Caring for something besides superficial small-talk and eating and drinking and banal amusements.

FATHER: (*Hurt, displeased*) Oh, right.

MOTHER: Come on, don't be silly. I wouldn't talk like that, Walt: it isn't nice. I'm sure there's not such a difference between us, us three—and your father— (*To* FATHER) We get on just the same as we ever did, don't we? What do you say, my old dear? I don't see any reason I should apologize for spending time with the children. (*More seriously*) You see, you could often do so much more for your fellow man if you had a deeper understanding of things....

FATHER: (*Who at first had nodded, satisfied and reassured, again a bit maliciously*) All right, but try and understand *me* for a change.

MOTHER: Don't we?

SON: (*Surprised*) Do you feel that we *don't* understand you?

FATHER: (*Peevish*) I know it. You talk a lot of bull. I am what I am, is that what you think? You don't suppose that there's anything special to understand.

MOTHER: (*Laughing, tips* SON *the wink, and at last he grins too; to her husband*) Now, let me get you another cup of tea.

FATHER: (*Laughing good-naturedly*) All right. (*Still seated, tapping his fingers on the table*)

SON: (*After a moment*) Hey, Father, will you please stop that tapping? It gets on my nerves.

FATHER: (*Stops, shaking his head, almost in despair*)..

MOTHER: (*Passing the tea, pacifying*) Let's play some cards. Hey? Walt? Since your father has his heart set on it.

SON: (*At a look from his mother; accommodating*) Well, go ahead then. I don't mind.

MOTHER: Say, Gerard, shall we...play some cards?

FATHER: Fine. Great. A hand of gin?

(SON *gets the cards.* MOTHER *puts aside the books and the paper.*)

(*Enter the* DAUGHTER.)

DAUGHTER: (*In hat and cloak; cheery*) Hello, father. Hello, mother dear. Hello, Walt.

FATHER: So. Right on cue. Want to join in? We can play something else. Bridge.

DAUGHTER: No. I'm staying just a second, you see. Any tea left, Mom? I just came to say that I have to go to Lucie's for a while.

MOTHER: Oh, why must you, Lisa? You're always in a hurry and never at home.

DAUGHTER: Don't exaggerate!

MOTHER: No, it's true!

FATHER: Lucie won't run away, will she! You stay and keep company with the old folks at home.

DAUGHTER: No, please, not this evening. (*Goes and sits on the arm-rest of her father's chair*) I think it's a shame. You're such a stick-in-the-mud with your card-playing, you old (*Kisses him on the head*) ...grouch! (*Kisses him again. Leaping up*) Now please, I have to go to Lucie's.

MOTHER: Any special reason?

DAUGHTER: (*Hesitant and looking at* SON) Oh, I don't know....

MOTHER: (*To* SON) Didn't you and Lucie have something on today? Didn't you go out for a walk this afternoon?

SON: With Lucie? Certainly not.

MOTHER: (*Reproachfully*) Come now, Lisa, why do you have to be so mysterious?

DAUGHTER: Well, you know...I'll only be out for a minute.

MOTHER: And afterwards?

DAUGHTER: For heaven's sake, mummy, why do you keep asking all these boring questions? I can't tell you. And I don't know anyway, so there. But don't worry about my going out.

FATHER: Oho, listen, that won't do! Is that a way to talk to your mother? You ought to have more respect, missie. If I'd behaved like that when I was your age! Yes, yes—you're always up to some foolishness!.. You want *me* to tell you what? If you and your mysteries can't stand the light of day, then you can stay home and that's that.

DAUGHTER: (*Rebelliously*) And I tell you again that I don't know why myself. *If* there's a mystery, then it's hers, not mine.

FATHER: (*Regarding it as craziness*) My, my—the girl's getting touchy!

MOTHER: Oh, Gerard, let it go. Girls are like that...you mustn't be too hard on her. Let her go now...

FATHER: (*Shrugging it off*) Well, go on then.

(*The telephone rings downstairs*)

DAUGHTER: The phone. Shall I see who it is?

FATHER: No, I suppose it's for your brother. It's rather late. (*Exits*)

DAUGHTER: Lucie's been crying.

MOTHER: Crying?

DAUGHTER: She wouldn't admit it or let me see, but I kept at her and when she looked at me, I could tell clearly: she'd been crying.

MOTHER: What about?

DAUGHTER: (*Shrugging her shoulders*) She wouldn't say. She tried to insist it was nothing. That's why I want to go to her now.

MOTHER: Dear, is that the right thing to do? Maybe she'd rather not have company. Or would she?

DAUGHTER: Yes, I think she'll be glad I came.

MOTHER: Well, all right, then you may go. (*To* SON) Do you suppose there's anything wrong? You talked to her this afternoon.

SON: (*Surly*) Hm!

DAUGHTER: Did she seem normal to you?

SON: I dunno.

MOTHER: Hey, what do you mean! You know very well.

SON: All right, I know very well. I...we had...ah, I can't tell you.

MOTHER: (*Laughing*) Goodness, Walt, I noticed a long time ago that Lucie had a thing for you, but are you just a little bit... in love with Lucie?

SON: (*Surly*) Absolutely not.

MOTHER: (*Dismayed*) Well—it wouldn't be a mortal sin.

SON: No, I know that. But I've told you already: I'll never get married.

MOTHER: People who talk like that are first to do it.

(FATHER *re-enters.*)

FATHER: (*In a hat, dressed to go out, in the doorway, to his wife*) I have to go out, it seems. Be back soon.

MOTHER: (*Following him*) Wait, dear, put on your coat. It'll be dark soon.

(SON *and* DAUGHTER *are left alone.*)

DAUGHTER: (*Goes to sit confidentially by* SON) So, Walt, can you tell me now?

SON: No, I can't.

DAUGHTER: Why not? You can trust *me*, can't you?

SON: Yes, but not about this.

DAUGHTER: You've been so grumpy lately. What's wrong with you? Is it to do with Lucie?

SON: No. —There's nothing wrong with me.

DAUGHTER: Yes there is. I've noticed it for a long time now. You'd better tell me, Walt. (*Silence*) —It's because you proposed to Lucie...

SON: Certainly not. Out of the question. Hey, don't you go thinking that too. It's too embarrassing for me.

DAUGHTER: Then are you...maybe...is there someone else?

SON: Not that either. —Definitely not!

DAUGHTER: Then what happened between you and Lucie? Was that why she was crying?

SON: I...I expect so.

DAUGHTER: She loves you.

(SON *is silent.*)

DAUGHTER: Does that make you uncomfortable?

(SON *nods yes.*)

DAUGHTER: Have you told her?

SON: No...or yes. I did tell her.

DAUGHTER: (*After a silence*) How awful for her, Walt, to have to hear that.

(SON *is silent.*)

DAUGHTER: Don't you feel anything for her? Or for the time being you...you could easily...

SON: No. I already told you: I'll never get married. She knows that.

DAUGHTER: Don't be stupid! Why not?

SON: Just because.

DAUGHTER: Do you have a special reason for it?

SON: Yes.

DAUGHTER: Then she knows...or thinks it's hopeless.

SON: She knows.

DAUGHTER: So you've told her the reason?

SON: Yes. I believe she has a right to that. Don't be cross with her because I can't tell you about it. It's nothing to do with marriage—

(DAUGHTER *shrugs.*)

SON: Ah, Lisa, if only you knew...I am so unhappy. (*Hides his face in his hands*)

DAUGHTER: (*Alarmed*) My God, Walt! You'd better tell me about it. Won't you?

SON: (*Shaking his head; jumps up*) I can't and I—I mustn't.

DAUGHTER: Mustn't?

SON: No—

DAUGHTER: Why not?

SON: A feeling I have. There are things I can't talk about to you, a girl.

(*Silence*)

DAUGHTER: But...but what if you told Charles?

(SON *laughs bitterly.*)

DAUGHTER: I don't understand. What dreadful thing all of a sudden... (*Hesitating*) I can ask Charles...

SON: (*Harshly*) Charles wants nothing to do with me.

DAUGHTER: But in the past...?

(SON *is silent, shrugging.*)

DAUGHTER: Did something happen between you and Charles...?

SON: No...

DAUGHTER: But in the past the two of you were inseparable.

SON: (*Entreating*) Please, Lisa...

DAUGHTER: I didn't say anything wrong, did I?

SON: (*Sighing*) Oh no. —Let's drop the subject.

DAUGHTER: That's what Charles says when I talk to him about it.

SON: Then *stop* asking.

(*Silence*)

DAUGHTER: All right—but I'm going over to Lucie's.

SON: Say, Lisa, would you do me a favor?

(*As* DAUGHTER *stares at him quizzically*)

SON: Don't ask Lucie the reason why...you know, what we were talking about.

DAUGHTER: (*Shrugging*) Fine.

SON: And don't bring it up again, hear.

DAUGHTER: I think it's too mean, all these secrets—

SON: Anyhow there are some confidences you and I can share... Tell me, do you...love Charles, hm?

DAUGHTER: (*Surprised*) What a question! Of course!

SON: What about him?

DAUGHTER: You mean: does he love me?

SON: Yes?

DAUGHTER: That goes without saying.

SON: So, you never had any doubts.

DAUGHTER: (*Hesitant*) No... Hey, Walt, don't be snide!...

SON: Lisa—honestly?!

DAUGHTER: I...I don't know. It's such a strange question. —Do you know something?

SON: No—

DAUGHTER: Then why do you ask?

SON: No reason. —Because...because of something I've noticed in you. If you... have doubts, Lisa, you'd better send him packing.

DAUGHTER: Walt! Are you crazy! (*Silence*) Charles loves me. I'm sure of it...I...I'm sure of it... (*Begins to weep*)

SON: (*Putting his arm around her shoulder*) Lisa, come on...

DAUGHTER: What is it—what have you...what do you know? Or what does Charles know? ...Why are you both so evasive?

(MOTHER *stands in the doorway.* DAUGHTER *exits quickly.*)

MOTHER: Walt, what is it now? —What's the meaning of *this* now?

(SON *is silent.*)

MOTHER: Walt, can't you answer?

SON: I...I don't know.

MOTHER: That's all we ever hear nowadays. You've got to stop being so dodgy, you hear. I insist on an honest answer. I'm your mother: don't I have a right to my children's trust?— All right, I know there are things you would rather keep for others, so I'm no closer to an answer. But enough is enough and now I want to know what's going on. (*Silence, gently*) Well, Walt?

SON: Oh dear, Mother, I can't tell you.

MOTHER: (*Simply*) Not your own mother? Is there *anything* you can't tell your mother? Haven't I done my very best to keep up with you, educate myself and try not to lag too far behind you? I never had the education you had. When I read books, I have no... no way to discriminate; I can't understand why you find some things so beautiful. But you know, Walt, I'm always willing to talk it over with you and often when I have things explained to me, I understand and find them beautiful too. —I have become better educated through you.

SON: Because it was latent in you.

MOTHER: That may well be. —But my intention was not to lose you, to behave so that you could always sit and talk to your mother about whatever was going on with you, your interests. —Especially when I saw, Walt, that you had a feeling for the arts. And as soon as I realized that, I talked your father into letting you take up music. There was a time when I wouldn't have done that; I would have sided with your father and said: learn a trade, art's a waste of time.

But I've grown closer to you, I keep trying to move forward with you and I have begun to understand so much more. It hasn't been easy... But that's not what I meant to say, Walt, because you know all about that: I live entirely in you and through you and for you as well...so do things have to be like this now? Am I now to be shoved aside and shut out, just like that?

SON: No, Mother, that's not what I mean, you mustn't take it like that. Lisa and I know perfectly well how you—well, how can I put it? how different you are from Father.

MOTHER: (*Mildly reproachful*) Your father loves you so much!

SON: Well yes, but he never understood you.

MOTHER: I know very well what you mean, my dear. —Anyway, let's not discuss it.

SON: And it's not that we don't trust you.

MOTHER: Then what?

SON: It's too hard to explain. I can't easily account for it myself.

MOTHER: Is it something to do with Lisa? Why was she crying?

SON: Because I... mentioned Charles.

MOTHER: What did you say about Charles?

SON: I asked if she was sure that he loved her.

MOTHER: You think he doesn't?

SON: (*After some hesitation*) Yes.

MOTHER: Why?

SON: Because... (*Falls silent*)

MOTHER: Now, Walt, you can trust me. Tell me everything.

SON: (*In doubt*) Everything? What if you don't understand? I don't entirely understand myself.

MOTHER: I will understand all right, dear—or else I'll learn to understand.

SON: You remember what Charles and I used to be like?

MOTHER: What do you mean? —Yes, something about your friendship did give me pause, something intense... Is that what you mean?

SON: Yes, you and I had lot of talks about it.

MOTHER: Yes, I couldn't help it. I think that sort of friendship, where you can't be without one another for a minute, is something, something...

SON: Unnatural.

MOTHER: Well, yes—that's it...

SON: You said so at the time and you remember how angry it made me?

MOTHER: Yes. I understand that too. You had no... impure intentions.

SON: No, not at the time. At least...

MOTHER: Walt! Why... (*Whispering*) what then?

SON: (*Weeping*) Mother, I'm too ashamed. You don't know what this does to me. And I am...I am not guilty....

MOTHER: How...do you mean that?

SON: It's not my fault. It was born in me.

MOTHER: (*Incredulous and indignant*) Born in you!

SON: I don't know how to put it. The fault is nature's. It is a curse hanging over me.

MOTHER: But Walter, my dear, I don't understand... how did you come to have such thoughts?

SON: Thoughts? —They *aren't* thoughts.

MOTHER: But you're not... Walt—you haven't...done things...

SON: (*Forcefully*) No. Don't think that about me.

MOTHER: But you said yourself: they aren't thoughts.

SON: No, they're not thoughts. They are...nature...or rather, unnature. But it's something that doesn't just inhere in thoughts or in actions either; it's something that fills my whole being, that lives inside me on its own and has lived in me from the day I was born.

MOTHER: (*Incredulous*) My dear! What nonsense!

SON: Mother, it's something I can do nothing about; something you must never reproach me for.

MOTHER: Of course I won't!

SON: No, that's not true. That's not what I mean. You don't have the right to reproach me...

MOTHER: In the first place, I have never done so...

SON: Not in the past, and that made me watchful and reticent. I started analyzing myself; I looked for the cause and—and I began to feel ashamed too. Oh, it's awful when you feel ashamed for something that's not your fault.

MOTHER: But for heaven's sake, Walt! When you became aware that you were going wrong...

SON: I didn't go wrong; I'm not going wrong. There's nothing else I can do.

MOTHER: But I don't understand, I still can't understand....

SON: I feel I...belong to another species.

MOTHER: Another spe... But Walt, you should be ashamed.... That's utter nonsense.

SON: Don't be so quick to say something is nonsense just because you don't understand it.

MOTHER: Shut your mouth!

SON: No, you wanted to hear this. This is the truth. Now I'll tell you. I've been beating around the bush and keeping silent too long. I really am glad you forced me to speak.

MOTHER: Oh! How horrible!

SON: But *not* wicked, mother, not wicked.

MOTHER: I...don't know that.

SON: I tell you it's born in one. It lives inside one.

MOTHER: Oh no it doesn't! How can that be! You must fight against it.

SON: I can't oppose my whole nature. You can't oppose the fact that you are a woman and feel and think like a woman.

MOTHER: My God, that is something entirely different.

SON: After all I got it from you and Father.

MOTHER: What are you saying...? For shame! How dare you!

SON: Because I was born of the two of you.

MOTHER: Yes, but... But that's no reason to shift the blame on us for everything you've done wrong.

SON: I've done nothing wrong and I don't shift *blame* on you.

MOTHER: Oh, God, Walt! I don't know what to say about all this. It's so taken me by surprise—but I find it—yes, I cannot help it, my dear, but I find it disgusting, abhorrent.

SON: It is that too.

MOTHER: Can't you do something about it, since you admit it yourself?

SON: If you only knew how I've tried! How I've fought against it! But it's nothing...wicked, nothing I can change. Nothing that I can discard and reform, because it's part and parcel of my soul. Yes, I don't know how I can explain it, but you might just as well say to me: breathing is bad for you; you must resist it.

MOTHER: No, no, that's where you're wrong. I'm afraid that you are being too easy on yourself. It is *always* painful to admit to bad habits and resist them. Everyone is quick to beg off, to say: I can't do anything about it, it's just a part of me.

SON: That's true, but believe me now, this really is too much a part of my being. So I can't do anything about it.

MOTHER: Oh, Walter! Now that you know how horrible I find it. I don't understand...don't understand.

SON: It is a curse, a crime against me.

MOTHER: Be quiet.

SON: Ha! Why?

MOTHER: You mustn't say such things.

SON: Then you should sing praises to Providence!

MOTHER: (*Sternly*) Walt, be quiet! I won't listen to that kind of talk.

SON: But if you only realized how it torments me! Then you yourself would rise up in rebellion. Faced with such...monstrous creations how can you still praise a righteous God!

MOTHER: (*Broken*) How bitter you are, my dear. —Wretched boy!

SON: Wretched, yes, that's the right word.

MOTHER: If only I could help—but I—I don't know what advice to give, I don't know any solution. I don't understand it. God, how can so many dreadful things come crashing down all at once? Just a moment ago we were still so happy.

SON: You were—I wasn't.

MOTHER: Oh, my boy... (*Pause*) I don't know about these things, Walt. —Maybe it's terribly stupid of your mother. I have never, even in my imagination, heard of such things. —But every so often these days you read about it in the papers. What's it called...?

SON: Homosexuality.

MOTHER: Yes, it's come to be considered a crime. Every day there are trials, criminal cases. It ends up in prison.

SON: It used to be considered a crime. But it is *not* a crime. It is something that demands the right to exist.

MOTHER: (*Hastily*) No. What is the world coming to if morals stand on such shaky ground? Everybody feels a natural antipathy to this sort of thing— (*Silence*) Walter, when I think of what you were like as a little child, cheerful, healthy, a little quiet perhaps, how cheerful and happy you always were, at home how you'd get wrapped up in your music and sing and play the piano. And to think that something so horrible could destroy that. I still can't imagine it: I can't get my head around it. Either it can't be true... (*Hopeful*) ...or else it will turn out to be a wicked fancy of yours.

SON: No, no—

MOTHER: How long have you known about it?

SON: Actually from the time I was twelve.

MOTHER: So long and you never spoke of it?

SON: I would never have been able to. Only now I understand that it was living inside me then; that I was different from other boys. I was not a boy.

MOTHER: (*Raising her hand to ward it off*) God, Walt, that sounds so unnatural, don't say things like that.

(SON *shrugs and is silent.*)

MOTHER: How can I begin to understand all this? Who can I talk it to about it? ...I don't know, I don't know.

SON: I don't know much about it myself; I wish I could find someone, an educated person you could talk to... Maybe Pastor Bruinsma.

MOTHER: No. Oh no!

SON: Why not? It is not sinful.

MOTHER: Maybe not—but I don't feel I can talk to Pastor Bruinsma about such things. A doctor instead—

SON: Do that then.

MOTHER: Maybe...

SON: So long as you don't talk to Father about it. Promise me that.

MOTHER: No, all right. Or actually—I don't know, Walt, whether I can do that. I'm obliged to inform your father.

SON: Oh, Mother, please, don't do it. That would be unbearable.

MOTHER: I'll see—I'll see about it. Let me think it over.

SON: Oh, no, I have to know....

MOTHER: Goodness, Walt, I'll do it so that your Father... God, I don't know how, but trust me.

SON: Father can be too rough.

MOTHER: He doesn't mean to be.

SON: No—but in this case I won't be able to bear it.

MOTHER: I can undertand that. I won't talk about it the same...the same way I do with you. After all I'm still too unfamiliar with the subject myself. (*Falls silent*) Is that the reason, Walt, why Charles is avoiding you?

SON: I think so—

MOTHER: Then he knows...?

SON: He will understand.

MOTHER: (*Hesitantly*) Should I...talk it over with Charles some time?

SON: Oh no, no. Definitely not.

MOTHER: Why do you think he doesn't love Lisa?

(*A silence*)

SON: Doesn't love her is not what I said.

MOTHER: Don't split hairs.

SON: Because... (*Shrugs and is silent*)

MOTHER: Well?

SON: I don't believe he proposed to Lisa because he loves her.

MOTHER: Why else? (*Since* SON *keeps silent.*) She has no money...

SON: Oh, no.

MOTHER: Does it have anything to do with...that?

SON: Yes—

MOTHER: How so? I don't understand....

SON: It's just a supposition. I may have noticed, earlier, that he...is just like me...perhaps, to a lesser degree.

MOTHER: (*More and more appalled*) Walter! No! That's horrible, what you just said. —Do you know it for a fact?

SON: No, I only fear it's so.

MOTHER: Then why should he want to marry Lisa?

SON: (*Shrugging*) To protect himself from himself, perhaps—or from the world...

MOTHER: (*Stammering*) Oh, no. Oh, no.

SON: I don't *know* it for a fact.

(*While* MOTHER *sits with her head in her hands, we hear* FATHER *come home, whistling.*)

MOTHER: (*Startled*) There is Father. What should I do? God, God, what should I do? I can't look him in the face right now. Or Lisa either. I have to recover first. —Tell him that I had a headache and went to bed. Good night, Walt! (*Strokes his hair*)

SON: (*Holding up his face*) Good night, Mother!

(MOTHER *gives* SON *a hesitant kiss. —She exits. —He looks after her, deeply hurt. —*FATHER *comes in whistling.*)

(*Curtain*)

END OF ACT ONE

ACT TWO

(The same room in the morning. DAUGHTER *sits day-dreaming by the window.* FATHER *comes in.)*

FATHER: Good morning, my girl. Where's your mother?

DAUGHTER: I dunno. In her room perhaps.

FATHER: Call her then.

(DAUGHTER *listlessly gets up.* FATHER *watches her attentively. As she walks past him, he takes her hand, seats her on his lap, where she remains aloof, withdrawn.)*

FATHER: (*Jovially, heartily*) My darling daughter!

(DAUGHTER *stares at him in surprise, with a forced smile.*)

FATHER: You can still sit on your father's lap, even though you're such a big girl! (*Pause—then gently, probing his memory*) Lisa, what games we used to play together, eh? Do you remember that? (*Pause*) You were still a toddler then.

DAUGHTER: (*Smiling dimly*) Yes.

FATHER: (*With forced liveliness*) Do you remember? Can you really remember? In summer, when we'd go to the tea plantation and I'd push you on the swing? I always played with, didn't I? And when you were still just a tot, you rode on a pony; do you remember that? (*Pause*) —Yeah—

DAUGHTER: (*Rises, with a flat, enigmatic laugh*) Where did that come from?

FATHER: (*Stroking his forehead with his hand*) I've been doing a lot of reminiscing.. (*Sighing*) You're grown up now—and so...

DAUGHTER: Yes, of course (*Arches her eyebrows in surprise, cheerfully*) Silly old Dad! Are you getting sentimental?

FATHER: You can give me a kiss! (*Embarrassed*) You really used to be crazy about me. (*Pause*) —Yes, times have certainly changed. Now give me... a big, wet kiss.

DAUGHTER: (*Embarrassed, half laughing*) Oh God, Father. —Why are you acting so strangely (*Laughing brightly*) Now there, you see. Stop looking so gloomy—

(DAUGHTER *gives* FATHER *a kiss; he kisses her heartily in return, then claps her on the shoulder.*)

FATHER: (*Loudly and cheerfully*) Everything all right, my girl? Now go call your mother.

(DAUGHTER *exits.*)

(FATHER *stares pensively out the window.*)

MOTHER: (*In the doorway*) Did you call me, Gerard?

FATHER: (*quickly turning around*) Come in, dear heart...

MOTHER: (*Nervous*) Yes, but... (*Comes in*)

FATHER: I just remembered: did you see the doctor again yesterday? Do you keep going there, because you think Walt's too high-strung? It actually slipped my mind yesterday, because I came back by the last train. What did the doctor say? Nothing out of the ordinary, I suppose?

MOTHER: (*Earnestly now and steady*) Yes, Gerard, it is something out of the ordinary (*She moves to a chair and sits.*) We have to have a serious talk about it.

FATHER: (*Uneasy*) What do you mean? Is it something that...unusual? Is it... What is it?

MOTHER: (*Nervous*) It's...it's...it's horrible.

FATHER: Horrible?

MOTHER: I mean...dangerous for...Walt.

FATHER: (*Leaping up*) What? And why did you wait so long to tell me?

MOTHER: (*Placating*) Not physical danger. —Moral danger—

FATHER: (*Somewhat reassured, surprised*) Moral danger?

MOTHER: (*Taking his hand*) Just listen, Gerard, you are...you're a little too quick-tempered, when there's something you don't understand...

FATHER: Has he been pulling some stupid stunt?

MOTHER: What do you mean?

FATHER: (*Shrugging, dourly*) The boy isn't...consorting with women, or anything like that?

MOTHER: No, he is still pure, physically. But his thoughts...

FATHER: (*Impatient*) Well, yes. —Every boy has that sort of thing at his age.

MOTHER: But it isn't normal. These are not normal sex drives, the kind that people act on. It is...

FATHER: Well, spit it out, damn it.

MOTHER: God, I don't dare say it all at once. (*Pause*) Don't you understand? You've read in the papers... about strange things...

FATHER: (*Who slowly begins to understand*) What! That's not what's wrong with Walt...?!

(FATHER *slams his fist on the table*—MOTHER *falls silent with bowed head.*)

FATHER: Are you crazy, woman? What's happened?

MOTHER: Happened—nothing.

FATHER: Then what's the matter?—

MOTHER: Not actions. Just thoughts. Sinful, or no... abnormal thoughts.

FATHER: Ah, what, thoughts! If nothing's actually happened, why are you making such a fuss? You were scaring me to death.

MOTHER: It is horrible enough as it is. The doctor said it proves that the boy has unnatural tendencies.

FATHER: How does he know that? Just from what you told him?

MOTHER: I told him how the boy thinks and feels...

FATHER: And that's enough for him to imagine that... that...

MOTHER: It is so, unless we shut our eyes to it. The doctor was positive.

FATHER: I don't believe it. Walt...you suggest...a thing like that... (*Paces up and down*) It's the goddamnedest thing I ever heard! ...It's the very worst thing you can think of.. And even though nothing has happened?— All because of thoughts!

MOTHER: Don't get all worked up now, Gerard. Believe me, it's not just mere supposition. I was with the doctor a very long time and he asked me about everything... I quite understand why you can't believe it...it stunned me too at first...it comes over you so suddenly, this... this calamity; but what's the good of trying to ignore it.... That's the way things are.... It really is the way things are....

(*Silence*)

FATHER: (*Resisting*) That's the way things are because of your damned education. It's poisoned his heart.

MOTHER: No, a thing like that is inborn.

FATHER: Don't try that on me! Inborn! The thoughts or whatever you call that airy-fairy drivel, they have to be inborn in him! What crap! God, I'm really glad that nothing's actually happened. —I'll take that young man in hand. I'll soon cure him of his fantasies.

MOTHER: They are *not* fantasies and it is *not* curable. The doctor explained it to me—

FATHER: Just leave it to me, I'll soon get Walter sorted out. He's doing it to spite you, honestly.

MOTHER: (*Gently*) You'd better try to understand. You know too little about it to able to condemn so quickly. —Walt is greatly to be pitied. —What a miserable life the child will have, always at odds with his own nature, always an outcast in the world, or living a lie. (*She weeps.*)

FATHER: I think you're raving. There's *nothing* to it. He hasn't done the slightest thing. —Thoughts—yeah, sure, thoughts! What a boy like that needs is a good talking-to and he'll get one, hot and heavy, too.

MOTHER: Oh no. If you don't believe me, Gerard, ask the doctor youself. (*After a silence*) You mustn't talk to Walter before you recognize that he is *not to blame*. I have sworn that myself.

FATHER: That's even lovelier! I'd like to see who's going to stop me.

MOTHER: I will.

FATHER: (*Laughs scornfully. Pause*) So you...you'd like me to put up with all this. —I am kindly requested not to get involved, I... Ah, all right, it's just as I suspected, but didn't want to admit. You and the children, you're a united front, but I (*Pause, sighing*) I'm always the outsider. I'm considered the ogre in my own house...

MOTHER: (*Frightened, warmly*) No, that's not true. Don't be unreasonable. —We are fond of you.

FATHER: I can't argue like you. I can't blabber about... feelings and thoughts. I'm a dumbbell, a dope, the average man. (*More gently*) But don't think (*Stammering*) that I don't feel, feel isolated because...for that very reason...many's the time... There!...

MOTHER: (*Fondly*) Gerard!

FATHER: I love you, what more can I do? ...There. —I'm not looking for pity... (*Paces up and down, finally stops in front of* MOTHER, *more sternly*) But it is hard, whenever you...every time you...take the side of the children this way.

MOTHER: (*Gently*) I have to do it... *He* has to be protected; and besides I am his mother.

FATHER: That's why you shouldn't be so blind and so ridiculously maudlin.

MOTHER: (*Earnestly*) I am not blind, but you are. Ah, my dear, wherever the boy may roam throughout the wide world, his parents should protect him. Let us be a haven where he is safe, where he can find unwavering trust.

FATHER: (*Shrugging*) Roam throughout the wide world! What's got into you? What is it really, after all? Nothing. A boy with hysterical ideas!

MOTHER: But the doctor said so too...

FATHER: Doctors talk too much. Nowadays they claim that every thief and murderer is sick. —Now if the boy had commited an offense, but thoughts... (*Makes a gesture of vagueness*)

MOTHER: Then promise me one thing: you won't talk to Walter about it until you've given it some thought. Believe me, you would alienate him for good and your harsh words will drive him exactly where you don't want him to go. —Stifle your objections and consult someone if you like. Just remember that you love

Walter and believe me, that is a good thing. That's what he needs, for he cannot do without love.

FATHER: It is my duty to be firm.

MOTHER: *Isn't* that being firm? You think that I'm weak with the children...

FATHER: In little things perhaps not...

MOTHER: The big things—ah, in those you are not so weak. —That's the cause of your isolation. —All that reading, for instance, that you scoff at so much; Walt's talent for music...those are the things you consider little and they are big. What you call my weakness is my strength.

(GERARD *shrugs silently and glumly. Pause*)

MOTHER: We have to discuss it together and try to understand...rationally... Then we might be able to guide Walter, deflect the dangers from him. At the moment we cannot do that; neither you nor I.

FATHER: And meanwhile the boy has to live with his mistakes—or deviation, or whatever you want to call it?

MOTHER: That can't be changed. We must let matters rest where they are.

FATHER: Good, I promise you I won't speak to him about it, so there! I'll take your advice and see the doctor myself— (*Falls silent*) —I only wonder: Don't things like that disgust you?

MOTHER: Disgust me? I have to force myself to be rational. My nature rebels; it makes me sick whenever I imagine...

FATHER: Well then...

MOTHER: But I also feel: I cannot condemn what is not a fault. That would be cruelty.

FATHER: Squeamish surgeons heal no wounds...

SON: (*Outside the door*) Lisa, are you there? are you upstairs? Play four-handed with me for a little while.

MOTHER: (*Quietly*) Remember what you promised me.

FATHER: Yes, all right—all right— (*He exits.*)

(*At the same time* SON *enters the room, with music in one hand and a little picture—a figure study of a female nude—in the other. He watches his* FATHER *walk away in silence, then stares at his* MOTHER, *understanding.*)

MOTHER: (*With forced cheerfulness*) What have you got there, Walt? (*Silence*) —How did you come by it? Let's see —

SON: Were you...talking about me?

MOTHER: After what the doctor told me, I couldn't avoid it—

SON: What did he say?

MOTHER: (*Hesitantly*) Dear, I hope that eventually Father will accept it with greater understanding. Naturally it overwhelmed him. First he has to get used to the horrible idea.

(SON *sneers.*)

MOTHER: *I* had to do the same.

SON: Ah! You or Father! What a difference!

(DAUGHTER *enters.*)

DAUGHTER: What is it? You want to play, Walt? ... Oh, what a charming picture! Whose is it?

SON: (*Smiling*) Mine. —Take a look at it, mother. How do you like it?

DAUGHTER: Beautiful! Charming! How did you get it?

SON: Bought it.

MOTHER: Bought it?

SON: Yes, with the money I got for my birthday from uncle Louis. Charming, isn't it, eh? —Look at the delicacy of this foot and arm, eh! It's done so lovingly, full of graceful contours. —And look at the curve of the profile,—and the expression on the face. There's an underlying sorrow to it— (*To the* MOTHER.) Do you think it's beautiful?

MOTHER: (*Hesitating*) Yes... Very beautiful—but...

DAUGHTER: But what?

MOTHER: (*Laughing*) I think it's absurd, Walt, to spend money on a thing like that!

DAUGHTER:	SON:
Why absurd?	Why's that?

MOTHER: Well, I don't know. —I have old-fashioned ideas.

SON: Still, I would like to hang it here in the living room.

MOTHER: Well—do as you like.

SON: To beautify the living room and make it attractive, mother. —I'd love to have a lot of beautiful things around me. If only Father doesn't think it's crazy. —Or—or... (*Looks at the* MOTHER)

MOTHER: Oh, not at all... Why should he? He doesn't have to think it as beautiful as you do. What does it matter?—I can't be all that enthusiastic myself...

SON: But you, mother... No, I'd rather take it upstairs to my own room. —He won't like it.

DAUGHTER: Hey—how can you be so sure....

MOTHER: Walt, you are being unfair, and harsh.

DAUGHTER: I think so too. Just the last few days I've been thinking you...your behavior is so hostile. Yes, it is, mother.

MOTHER: I believe that we've done wrong, we've been mean without wanting to..

SON: How so?

MOTHER: In every way. —We are too prone, my dear, to disrespect someone who has a cruder personality than we do. We have not respected your father.

SON: (*Somewhat annoyed*) Is that so!—Don't you think father...

MOTHER: Oh yes, I think we have, without meaning to. —We have been unfair to your father; he must suffer in his isolation!

SON: His isolation!

MOTHER: He's felt it keenly—more keenly than we have, that he is often shut out...

SON: Did he complain about that?

MOTHER: Complain, no. He said so.

DAUGHTER: (*Sighs*) It is true, Walt—he does feel it.

SON: What do you expect? He always insists everything is crazy and outrageous and I don't know what. He has never tried to meet you halfway or acknowledge any opinion other than his own.

MOTHER: That never used to bother you before. He has always been that way.

SON: Yes, all right—but we are older now.

MOTHER: Now you two are older... So we must be tolerant. —I know exactly what you're feeling and what you're driving at, but he cannot help it. He has stayed just as he was. I haven't. I have grown along with you—but we must not leave him behind. We are the more mature ones, we are capable of *seeing things his way*, and we must be careful not to reproach him.

SON: When have we ever reproached him? Never, so far as I know.

MOTHER: Not in words. But we let him know that he is different from us.

SON: Well, all right—I don't believe that ever bothered him.

MOTHER: It has. —I have felt it just now too acutely... that we have been unfair.

DAUGHTER: How weird, that father suddenly... worries about it so much. Just now he was on about me, about when we were little. When we were so nice to him.

MOTHER: It's really my fault...

SON: Oh, mother, don't be silly! (*Thinking it over*) Why hasn't he once tried to understand us a bit more.

MOTHER: You're asking him to give what he doesn't possess. No, it is up to us, to me above all to meet him halfway, to smooth over the differences.

SON: Everybody has a right to live his life his own way.

MOTHER: Nobody has the right to force another person to make sacrifices.

SON: And while you make allowances and exercise restraint, while you try to share father's bottom-feeding life and never let him know that you really desire something better, does he ever make sacrifices for you?

MOTHER: (*After some thought*) No, I don't think so. But I'm the one who benefits. You're not old enough to understand that yet. Anyway, this is more my business than yours. I only ask you, you in particular, Walt! to be kinder to your father. Live your own life, since you're young. But even if he doesn't understand your thoughts and actions, let him feel that you still love him, that he hasn't forfeited your affection. That will be enough.

DAUGHTER: (*Warmly*) There's no one like you! Darling!

SON: It's lucky that we have you. If you had ever argued for father's point of view,... I might have been able to see things his way.

MOTHER: Walt! Really!

DAUGHTER: Hey, don't exaggerate. —But it is depressing sometimes...for instance when you speak your mind or offer an opinion about something that you consider...sacred, and then father comes along with his belittling or sarcastic remarks, it gets you down...

SON: It drives you crazy, furious, just because you can't do anything about it, you can't hurt him back. —You know, when you don't answer back, so he thinks you don't resent it inside, and he thinks he's in the right! And you have to admit he's right—

MOTHER: So what?

SON: I don't understand how you can feel that way. You have your own firm convictions. *Yours* must be less resolute than mine.

MOTHER: (*Smiling*) I think so too, children. Mine take life into consideration, my wisdom is more experienced than yours. Later you'll understand what I mean. Youth is cruel and selfish—

SON: I don't see it as selfishness—but as a right.

MOTHER: Later on you won't insist so much on your rights. But just try once, Walt, to do what I ask.

SON: (*Muttering*) I *will*, but it's not easy.

DAUGHTER: You still want to play?

SON: Yes—in a little while.

DAUGHTER: All right, first I'll go to the office and bring father the mail. In a little while then. I'll be right back. (*She exits.*)

MOTHER: And that little picture, Walt, what will you do with it now?

SON: I'm afraid that now Father knows—that he—that he will think it... So, let me take it with me— (*As she is silent, snappishly*) You see, now it's starting.

MOTHER: What's that, my dear?

SON: The hiding, the dissembling, or whatever you want to call it, the inability to be honest, otherwise you get kicked, thrown out...

MOTHER: No, no, dear, why? Don't exaggerate. No matter what it's like for anyone else, here you must feel safe. You're at home here.

SON: But Father! He thinks I'm so wicked...

MOTHER: Wicked! You're his own child.

SON: But what does he say?

MOTHER: He can't adjust to this kind of situation. Not yet, at least—

SON: Never. —Oh, no—never!

MOTHER: All right, but don't expect quick results. And then—Walt—you will have to put up with prejudice from so many people once they know about it. — Therefore, dear, you must keep quiet, never mention it to anyone.

SON: I know that perfectly well. I'm always thinking about it, all the time. —Everyone ought to know— everyone ought to know. —I don't have it in me to be a hypocrite.

MOTHER: You are not a hypocrite—just because you don't talk about things.

SON: Oh, but keeping silent is no *easy matter*. It means keeping silent about your true nature, your whole inner being. It is a continual, everlasting silence. You think there is any time when I'm not aware, when I don't remember that I am different from how I ought to be, that I'm the way I'm not supposed to be...?

MOTHER: (*Frantic*) The world is cruel, my dear, that's true! You cannot defy it. It is a good thing that no one knows about it. You know what the doctor says: thre most important thing is to keep it a secret. You have never spoken to *anyone* about it, have you, Walt?

SON: Only Lucie.

MOTHER: (*Alarmed*) Lucie? How could you be so...

SON: Oh—but she'll keep quiet. —Mother, I have heard the bell ring twice. Shall I?...

MOTHER: No, let me... (*Exits*)

(*Enter* FIANCÉ.)

FIANCÉ: (*Upset*) Walter, I have to talk to you.

SON: (*Jumping up, alarmed*) What is it? What's the matter?

FIANCÉ: I am desperate.

SON: What is it...what have you... Where is Lisa?

FIANCÉ: (*Falling on to a chair*) Lisa, she's with your father...at the office...

SON: (*Somewhat relieved*) God...you scared me.... What is it?

FIANCÉ: I...I haven't got the nerve to say it right out, Walt...Lisa is too dear to me...and I....I can't keep it up, Walt; I feel as if I'm choking...but then—I want to. Oh, Walt, I want to with every ounce of will power I've got—

(SON, *eyes cast down, remains silent.*)

FIANCÉ: Why don't you say something?

SON: I was afraid of this.

FIANCÉ: (*Alarmed, suspicious*) What?

SON: (*On the point of betraying himself*) That you...

FIANCÉ: Well?

SON: (*Dully*) That you—don't love Lisa enough.

FIANCÉ: (*Back-peddling*) Well... I don't know. I love Lisa dearly, believe me, Walt, I do love her... a lot...

SON: Like a little sister perhaps.

(FIANCÉ *is silent—looking at him more quizzically.*)

SON: But to become man and wife...

FIANCÉ: You know—that's just it—whenever I think about it... (*Falls silent.*)

SON: Well, say it; I understand you better than you think.

FIANCÉ: (*Bursting out*) I don't know what it is, Walt. Every kiss, every caress...that I take...or she asks for... Oh, I tell you, I do love her; I care for her...

SON: You must be strong and call it off, Charles.

FIANCÉ: No—

SON: If not for yourself, then do it for her. Break off this engagement, you...it's the only thing to do!

FIANCÉ: (*At the other end of the room, away from* SON, *whispering rapidly*) Walt, you don't understand me...or do you?

SON: (*Looking at him*) Yes, completely. I believe that our friendship of old, not that there was anything...wrong about it...we were able to understand one another...

FIANCÉ: So you too...I thought so. That's why I didn't trust you; for I was afraid that I would betray myself, you might notice something abnormal in my dating

Lisa, or whatever and...and I was ashamed to get engaged. But you knew all about it, didn't you?

SON: I had a strong suspicion.

FIANCÉ: And I sensed that you knew it. I could have hated you for it. But now I am glad that I can speak out about it. —God, for once someone who understands; who I know will not condemn me. I have struggled... This engagement period is hell for me...and then, I hoped, Walt, that if I could just hold out...that I could get a grip on myself, that perhaps I could become like everybody else.

SON: How could you do that, you who has such an aversion to...

FIANCÉ: Quiet...don't say it out loud—

SON: And then...think of Lisa. You can't just consider yourself. —You're sacrificing someone else.

FIANCÉ: But maybe...perhaps—in time I...

SON: No. You would only make Lisa miserable.

FIANCÉ: I am afraid of myself—and of the world—of... especially of being alone in it. —Don't you feel that way? Always alone—apart from others—Never anyone who really loves you, so long as you are... Can you stand that?

SON: (*With quiet pride*) I have my mother.

FIANCÉ: Are you sure? Have you told her and *she* understands?! (*Gently*) Then you're lucky. And your father, have you told him as well?

SON: No, but he knows it...sorry to say.

FIANCÉ: Sorry to say?

SON: (*Shrugs his shoulders*)

FIANCÉ: I don't believe anyone can forgive it.

SON: Forgive!

FIANCÉ: Oh well... (*Listening*) Is anyone there? I'll go, Walt. Let me go before someone comes in here.

SON: Someone's going upstairs, that's all.

(FIANCÉ *and* SON *hear* DAUGHTER *singing as she goes upstairs.*)

SON: Is it agreed, Charles, that you'll break it off? Promise me—

FIANCÉ: God, no...

SON: (*Urgently*) I insist on it.

FIANCÉ: I'll see.... Don't tell anyone, and especially not Lisa....

SON: Put an end to it.

FIANCÉ: Yes, yes—but give me time...and promise me...

SON: I won't tell.

FIANCÉ: Thank you—

(FIANCÉ *and* SON *exit.*)

(FATHER *comes in, first looks out the window, then stands in front of the mirror, smoothes his moustache, sees the picture on the mantelpiece and stares at it in shock. —*MOTHER *comes in.*)

FATHER: Say, what's this cockeyed thing doing here? Is it supposed to be a conversation piece?

(SON *comes in.*)

MOTHER: Walter bought it.

FATHER: (*Grumbling a greeting*) Did you buy that thing?

SON: Yes. Do you find it ugly? Then I'll put it in my room.

FATHER: (*Angrily*) No, certainly not. You will not put it in your room. Filthy swine, what do you...

(SON *abruptly turns around.* MOTHER *comes between them.*)

MOTHER: Gerard, how can you be so... What's the matter with that picture! (*To* SON) No, Walt, don't lose your temper —

SON: (*Shrugging*) I told you so.

FATHER: What did you tell her?

SON: That you would think it was crazy.

FATHER: Crazy? No, not crazy, but shameless. —Just like you—of course you would have to...

(*A cry from* MOTHER)

SON: Well? What were going to say? Eh?

FATHER: Will you shut your impudent mouth?

SON: Say it now. —Go ahead. —You think I don't know!?

FATHER: All the better. Then I don't have to say it to you.

MOTHER: Walter, oh do go away. Leave the room.

FATHER: Here—take this thing with you.

SON: (*Flinging the picture in pieces at his feet and trampling on them*) There, there you've got what you want. That's what you like to do, eh? Trample on whatever's sacred to someone else...

FATHER: (*Laughs*) Sacred! I didn't know that *you* had a soft spot for women...

(FATHER*'s laughter turns to anger, as he sees that* SON *is about to defy him.* —FATHER *and* SON *stand facing one another.*)

(DAUGHTER *opens the door and stands there speechless.*)

MOTHER: (*Shoves away* SON, *who tumbles helplessly on to a chair, grabs hold of* FATHER, *almost weeping*) No! you're being a bully, a bully. Don't touch him, I say. I won't have it. (*Stands in front of* FATHER)

FATHER: (*Looking at the two of them; his anger ebbing away*) So! isn't this lovely! Go and take his side! (*To* DAUGHTER) Out of my way—let me by! Go to your brother and your mother, then the whole team'll be together. (*Walks out the door*)

MOTHER: Ah children!...

(*Curtain*)

END OF ACT TWO

ACT THREE

(FATHER, *after a look over his shoulder, stands whistling at the window.* —MOTHER *enters to set the breakfast table. She looks sad.*)

FATHER: So, finally somebody shows up! What a god-forsaken, depressing mess! Oh, for the love of God, do you have to look so glum all the time?

MOTHER: (*Abruptly*) Oh—Gerard...

FATHER: (*Mimicking*) Oh, Gerard... God, it makes me want to puke. Just when does the period of mourning end?

MOTHER: For heaven's sake...there's good reason for it....

FATHER: What! for always being so down in the mouth? Don't get me wrong, but I just can't see it. —As far as I can tell, taking one thing with another, you've got no cause to complain. You've got no worries, a husband who loves you, healthy children...

MOTHER: Healthy children!

FATHER: (*Emphatically*) Definitely—

MOTHER: How can you say that now? What about Walt?

FATHER: The doctor said himself that the boy is perfectly healthy.

MOTHER: Yes. Physically—

FATHER: No, morally too. —It is not a sickness. I spoke to the man myself; I know it now. — It's something quite different. —He's different from other people.

MOTHER: You're taking it rather lightly, at present. It doesn't sound like you.

FATHER: I'm not so stupid as to think I know better—yes, I know, I denied it at first, but I admit I was wrong. —When I realize that someone knows more about something than I do, I accept it politely.

MOTHER: You accept whatever is easiest.

FATHER: Nothing's ever good enough for you. First you wanted to convince me, like it or not, that someone like Walt is not depraved, but simply different from other people, but when *I* say it, you have to start an argument.

MOTHER: Oh no, I don't mean it like that, but you act as if it were nothing. His being different condemns him to a whole life of...abuse, loneliness.

FATHER: Never mind, so long as he takes care nobody finds out that he's so... peculiar, no one will be any the wiser.

MOTHER: What a way to live!

FATHER: Don't exaggerate. He has us—he can stay at home...

MOTHER: But—the greatest thing in a person's life, love, he'll be missing.

FATHER: He won't want it, will he? —

MOTHER: He...certainly will want it—

FATHER: Ah! What bull!

MOTHER: I don't understand you. —First you were entirely against it and now, now you accept it as if it were perfectly ordinary.

FATHER: I simply went to see your doctor. As he just said: it is inborn and you have to accept it—well, that's what I'm doing. —And I say: it's a lucky thing it doesn't affect his health. And, then again: nobody has to know. Things can go on as normal, the doctor told me, but nobody needs to talk about it.

MOTHER: (*Shrugging her shoulders*) You don't want to see. You want to be blind—

FATHER: And you don't want to be happy. You want to be miserable.

MOTHER: I can't be happy when my child is doomed to loneliness.

FATHER: But, my God, why should he be? —The boy will stay a bachelor. There's plenty of happiness outside of marriage. Just look at all the unmarried girls; their mothers don't die of chagrin.

MOTHER: That is different.

FATHER: How so?

MOTHER: In the first place, because it is open and honest. —This involves constant lying. It can destroy a life—

FATHER: Come on, destroy! Always the big words.

MOTHER. And then you forget: a girl who stays a wall-flower while life passes her by, always waiting, that is tragic too.

FATHER: Listen, if you start thinking like that, there's tragedy wherever you look.

MOTHER: Well, there is.

FATHER: God, woman, if that's how your mind works... How can a person change so much!.. These last few days, damn them.

(MOTHER *is silent.*)

FATHER: (*Pacing up and down*) I keep wondering how this began? Honestly, I sort of feel that as time goes by we keep moving farther away from one another, or, to be more precise, you've moved away from me, for I've stayed the same, always.

MOTHER: (*Gently conceding*) Yes, that is so—

FATHER: Then why do you do it? Why don't you stay the same as you've always been?

MOTHER: I can't help it. It's beyond me. Something in me has to be...consummated.

FATHER: Here we go again with the big words: consummated! You never used to talk like that.

MOTHER: (*Pondering*) No. I've been thinking about it a lot lately. (*Falls silent*) I realize I am not the way I used to be.

FATHER: You see. It's not so hard to change.

MOTHER: (*Shaking her head*) I'm no longer capable of it. And the children... Walt anyhow... if I should lose him because of it.

FATHER: (*Surprised*) Eh? What for?

MOTHER: I might not understand him.

FATHER: Oh, God! That constant *understand*!

MOTHER: He wouldn't have my support as he has it now.

FATHER: I expect he'll go his own way perfectly well. He knows better than his parents now.

MOTHER: Ah, come, he's just being his age and besides, they are better educated than we are; they are more cultured and they have modern ideas.

FATHER: Fine ideas!

(MOTHER *sighs and is silent.*)

FATHER: (*Irritated*) Why did you sigh just now?

MOTHER: (*Frightened*) God...

FATHER: Well?

MOTHER: (*Hesitantly*) I was thinking that you don't ever let them...

FATHER: So little by little you're beginning to think me the same dope my children do, eh? Best way to treat a fellow like that is let him talk, don't bother answering back. —So little by little you're ashamed that you've got such an idiot for a husband...

MOTHER: (*Protesting*) But Gerard...

FATHER: You think I don't feel it? You don't like me any more. Are you a wife? You lie next to me like a stone statue lately. Even a kiss is too much for you...

MOTHER: Don't you understand why?

FATHER: No, I don't understand, I never understand anything!

MOTHER: How can I be happy while I'm thinking of my boy, who will have to be always alone, lying and struggling? It seems too callous—it hurts me.

(FATHER *makes a feeble gesture of incomprehension.*)

MOTHER: I know all about your rights. I am your wife...

FATHER: What harm do you do the boy by it?

MOTHER: You are right, but...I would not be able to be happy with you. —Maybe if you felt the way I do, if there were no gulf between you and Walter, if you accepted it as an affliction, a misfortune...

FATHER: (*Discouraged*) Yes well, in other words, if I was something I'm not.

MOTHER: Oh no. Please believe that I love you—

FATHER: I don't know that. Sometimes...I don't believe it any more.

MOTHER: Oh, Gerard, what do I have to say? How can it be that what should bring us closer is driving us apart? ...I feel so lost...I can't put it into words. I...I feel such pity...for you too. But the pity for Walt swallows up everything, it's the most important thing. Maybe this time I am more mother than wife, but—let me be that way, for Walter needs it...

FATHER: What about me? Don't I need it?

MOTHER: You are no longer a child.

FATHER: The children are grown up now and will go their own way and in a couple of years the two of us will be left alone...

MOTHER: (*Frightened*) Alone...

FATHER: And I feel just as close to you as before, wife

(FATHER *puts his arm around* MOTHER *and tries to kiss her.*)

MOTHER: (*Gently fending him off*) Now, now, Gerard.

FATHER: (*Rudely*) Then go to hell, you and your son... (*Walks off in a huff*)

(MOTHER *stands still, rapt in thought, and then begins to lay out the dishes.*)

(*Enter* SON.)

SON: Morning, mother (*Sits at the breakfast table*)

MOTHER: (*Pouring out a cup of tea*) Morning, Walt. How late you are. You mustn't get up so late, I don't think it's right.

SON: Is Father gone already?

MOTHER: Walt, show some consideration and come to breakfast on time.

SON: Oh Mother, I never eat breakfast.

MOTHER: You mustn't be so lazy.

SON: I'm not lazy. I come a little bit later, when father is gone and I can sit and socialize alone with you.

MOTHER: For heaven's sake, Walt!

SON: Why do you always find fault with whatever I do?

MOTHER: What happened to the forbearance you promised me?

SON: It can't be produced on cue, you act as if I'm the parent and Father is still a child—

MOTHER: Ah...he really is a child. He always stayed a child.

SON: How could you have married Father! I don't understand it.

MOTHER: Why, Walt!

SON: That's what you always say: Why, Walt!

MOTHER: What sort of a question is that?

SON: Well, I'm used to it. You are quite a special person.

MOTHER: I have changed, my dear, especially lately, but your Father hasn't.

SON: I can't imagine that. You must always have been special.

MOTHER: That may be so, but if so, I was unaware of it. But that doesn't matter much, don't you find? I love him just as much as before and you were rather fond of him when you were still little.

(SON *shrugs his shoulders.*)

MOTHER: Well, after you told me that...that you hated him, Walt, I've been thinking— You have to...fight against it. — He is your father.

SON: (*Bitterly*) My father behaves to me the way the world will behave to me. —Everything's all right, so long as I think and act under cover, but the heavens fall the minute a person dares admit what he is, the minute I reveal anything about myself.

MOTHER: That isn't true. He loves you in his own way.

SON: (*Half involuntarily—half ashamed*) Is Lisa out?

MOTHER: Yes—

SON: Have you heard anything from Charles yet?

MOTHER: After that letter, you know the one, where he asks her to let him be by himself for a while, nothing more.

SON: It's beastly—

MOTHER: It won't go on much longer. He has to come to a decision. She can't put up with it much longer this way.

SON: If only she would make the decision.

MOTHER: (*Shaking her head*) No, that's not her place. It isn't up to her— (*Hesitantly*) I was thinking, Walt.... Could you talk to him again...? But then... Maybe not...

SON: (*Suspicious*) Why are you so hesitant? Do you suspect me of something?

MOTHER: (*Confused*) Goodness, my dear—no...

SON: Then why?

MOTHER: I think...I know...I trust you all right...but what do I know about Charles? And...and besides, I am worried that you are not guarded enough in the way you express yourself...and he might realize...

SON: What I'm like! What difference does it make, he's known for a long time, because I told him.

MOTHER: That isn't true!

SON: So what! He won't tell anyone else. —And even if he did: (*More quietly*) everyone knows it already, Mother...

MOTHER: (*Aghast*) What are you saying?

SON: You think that's so bad? I'm almost glad of it, now that it's over and done with. —I'd like—God—I'd like to shout it from the housetops. No more hypocrisy, no more lying.

MOTHER: Walt! Are you crazy?

SON: I want to live the way I am, the way Nature or God made me. —I dare to... (*More quietly*) ...because... I still have you, Mother.

MOTHER: (*Moved*) Oh Walt, my child!

SON: I am what I am and I am going to go through life open and forthright. Don't worry—I won't turn degenerate or hang out with bad characters, as the doctor warned. —Don't you feel, Mother, that it's much more honorable to stop the hypocrisy? I don't want to be humiliated or deny my nature, I refuse flat out, I won't do it—

MOTHER: Walter!

SON: I told the doctor—and yesterday the pastor as well.

MOTHER: The pastor? You were there?

SON: Yes. —He had asked me to come by.

MOTHER: (*Anxiously*) But what for?

SON: Don't you understand? I did it right away. He had heard rumors, he was on the alert and he felt called upon to separate the sheep from the goats.

MOTHER: Oh Walt! That's awful!

SON: Why? I satisfied his curiosity.

MOTHER: And what did he say? He will keep quiet? He has to keep quiet as pastor—

SON: Let him talk: it doesn't matter to me. That's what I told him.

MOTHER: But, for heaven's sake, Walter, that can't... How does he know? How do they know...?

SON: Lucie told her mother. Now, you understand: Madam told Sir, and Sir told a friend, and so on and so forth, and someone told the pastor. —That's the way things go around here! Rumors spread like wildfire.

MOTHER: Oh God...

SON: Is this then the worst you can imagine—the world's contempt? Isn't it enough that I have such an infinitesmal chance at happiness—that my life will pass like a dream—unreal—? That I am doomed to... loneliness? Never a family—never children—what does a little scandal matter compared to that? Are you that ashamed of me?

MOTHER: Oh no, my dear, I'm not... But...what will your father say when he hears of it?

SON: (*Toughing it out*) I don't know.

MOTHER: Don't act so indifferent, dear, I can't stand that.

SON: I want to be indifferent, to everything, everyone. Except you—Mother. But if it makes you sad, then it becomes a question of life and death to me. This hypocrisy is driving me frantic; I feel it; it's gnawing at me—it wears me down, it eats away at my self-respect.

MOTHER: What does Pastor Bruinsma say?

SON: Yes, what does he say? I don't know any more. He was outraged and called it a sin and a shame. A person like me is dangerous... A little understanding—or even a bit of tolerance—not a word of that.

MOTHER: Not everyone is the same. —You know, dear, most people don't take the trouble to *find out* first before they condemn—they feel aversion and that is natural and understandable too.

SON: We also have a right to live. It isn't fair to ostracize us and force us to deny ourselves. I don't understand, Mother, how so vast a prejudice can take root. —It is scientific knowledge that this is not a defect, it is a fluke of nature.

MOTHER: That may well be. —But whenever I visualize it, Walt! then I have to, I can't help but find it repulsive. —And I know that's, ah, it is hard for you, but in that respect I'm not so very unlike the society that condemns you.

SON: Mother!

MOTHER: It is a hatred born of the urge to procreate. My nature tries to resist it, but that's because you are my child. So if I condemn you, the condemnation is even harsher. No—be still, my dear! I know that it is unfair of society to condemn, but I can understand, Walter, why it has to be unfair. Because, even though you are my own child, I have to suppress my feelings before I can...

SON: Accept it?

MOTHER: But, my dear, I don't condemn it any more. I won't be able to do that now. I feel too much pity for you, poor boy.

SON: Oh no, Mother, most people are more to be pitied than I am—for I have you.

(Silence. Then the doorbell rings. MOTHER *exits.)*

FIANCÉ: (*Appears in the doorway*) Lisa is still not home, eh?

SON: No, Lisa is out.

FIANCÉ: (*Upset*) I 'd like to ask you, you see, if you would give her this letter, then you could prepare her... smooth the way...and explain...whatever you think needs explaining...

SON: So—you're calling it off...

FIANCÉ: Yes. (*After a silence, dejected*) I can't keep it up any more.. You have to explain...that I am not a bad person. I've been rather inconsiderate and cruel. I hate that. I have hurt her a lot, Walt. But...you don't know—God—you don't know. Try to explain...God no...don't explain... Let her think instead that I'm a bad person, otherwise she might understand and that, Walt, mustn't happen. —No one must know why... promise me that, won't you?

SON: All right.

FIANCÉ: Think me a coward...

(DAUGHTER *pushes the door open, throws her arms around* FIANCÉ*'s neck.*)

DAUGHTER: Charles! No... (*Silence, as she sobs*)

SON: (*Gently*) Lisa—darling.

DAUGHTER: (*Resisting desperately*) Oh no, let me. (*To Charles*) I watched until you came out of your house. And I followed you. First you asked if I was at home... but me—you didn't want to see me. —Oh, I understand. Now you want... Walt...to tell me... but I don't want to lose you... I cannot... I love you... (*Tries to hang on his neck. Charles recoils aghast, fending her off.*)

SON: (*Indignant, commanding her*) Lisa! Come here (*More tenderly*) It...it's better if Charles goes away.

DAUGHTER: First I want to know why. I want to know it from his own lips.

FIANCÉ: (*Broken*) Lisa, I wrote to you. I...I am not worthy of you.

DAUGHTER: (*Laughs*) Not worthy! What difference can that make to me! That's all very well in a novel. Tell me if you love me.

FIANCÉ: (*Gently*) No—I don't love you—not as much as you should be loved (*He runs out.*)

DAUGHTER: (*Sits numb, then to* SON) Give me—well—the letter—but.

SON: (*Handing over the letter, while Lisa sits and then gets up, moving away from him as she reads*) Do you want me... Do you want me to stay here...with you? (*As she shakes her head no*) or shall we both go upstairs, Lisa dear?

DAUGHTER: (*Blankly*) No, not that either. I want to be alone. (*She exits.*)

(SON *crosses to the window and looks out of it. Enter* FATHER.)

FATHER: Aha, so, you're here. The very man I want.

(MOTHER *comes in, frightened by his tone of voice.*)

FATHER: Dammit, a fine kettle of fish! Do you know who just came to see me at the office?

SON: (*Automatically*) Pastor Bruinsma.

FATHER: And you can say it like that? So calmly?

SON: (*Confused*) He told me that he was going to see you.

FATHER: Well, and?

SON: What and?

FATHER: Oh, you suppose I don't care? The whole town spits at you and points fingers at you. And I don't care? Doesn't it matter to you? Well, it does to me, it does to me—I have always been known around here as an upstanding decent man. I have never had anything to do with immorality.

SON: You still haven't.

FATHER: Haven't I? What about you? Someone of your type?

MOTHER: Quiet! (*Entreating*) Please, don't say such things.

SON: You know it then?

FATHER: Do I? Yes, and that was fine. Nobody else knew it; you were supposed to keep your mouth shut. We all impressed it on you, me, your mother, the doctor. But you, you go around talking about it, you take pride in it...

SON: That isn't true. I just don't want to be ashamed—

FATHER: That's it, that's it! Shamelessness, brazen shamelessness! Just what Pastor Bruinsma says. — People like you are the rot in the community and he must warn other youths against associating with you. (*To* MOTHER) Well, what do you say now? Are you convinced now, you, with your weakness and your tolerance? The rot in the community! And everyone will know it, already knows it. I see it in the way they greet me in the street, I hear them gossip at the office. My good name is gone. My name, that no man could say a word against, that I have upheld, until you... In the mud! The finger pointing...

MOTHER: Calm down! God, calm down a little, Gerard.

FATHER: (*Goes and sits—deliberately calm, to* SON) You—you know what sort of catastrophe you've caused here? You've ruined my good name, you've wheedled your mother away from me, your future brother-in-law shuns the house, because of you, because of what people say about you, naturally...

MOTHER: That isn't true, Gerard!

FATHER: Your sister's unhappy and you, you are the cause of it all— (*Stands up*) But you are leaving! You are leaving this house and you will be under strict supervision, I'll see to that. And there's an end to all that damned reading and drivel and sentimental music-making. I'll knock your abnormal fantasies out of your head. You'll get a job, a trade, like everyone else, and then we shall see if you can become a normal person.

MOTHER: For heaven's sake, Gerard, don't talk such nonsense.

FATHER: Nonsense? I've listened to your nonsense long enough. But now it's my turn. And you keep your mouth shut, from now on, about your so-called deviation! —Understand?

SON: No, spare yourself all the trouble, father, it doesn't help. You know that it is not a disease..

FATHER: It is rubbish. Disgusting, absurd crap!

SON: Call it whatever you like.

MOTHER: Walter, you'd better keep quiet.

FATHER: That's an order.

SON: I won't.

(*Gesture of entreaty from* MOTHER)

SON: Really, I cannot! Deny myself—I cannot. Nor do I want to.

MOTHER: You're are making things worse— You're pitting the whole world against you.

SON: So be it. —But I'm true to myself. What do I care about friendship, it's an illusion. A fraud, a cheat, that's what I think. People have to know! Oh, ever since I've stopped lying, I feel freer, healthier—

FATHER: Walter, I warn you! You can choose: Obey me and keep your mouth shut, or you can hit the streets for good and I...I wash my hands of you.

MOTHER: Walt! Give in, give in! —

SON: (*Dully*) I shall go, Mother. Do you want me to be a fraud as well?

MOTHER: Gerard! Think of it—he has no one. (*Pause*) Walter! I am on your side... Yes, I'll go with you if you have to go. And if the whole world is against him and despises him—I won't. I have faith in him.

SON: (*Kisses her hands*) Dear, oh dear Mother!

FATHER: (*Helplessly—unemphatic*) Don't push me to the limit. I order you both: you will stay here and you will keep quiet.

(*Enter* DAUGHTER.)

DAUGHTER: (*Looks round, blankly to the others*) I expect you know it already. —It's over between Charles and me.

FATHER: Over? So, he's called it off now? (*To* SON) You hear that? —And what reason does he give?

DAUGHTER: No reason. (*To* SON) But you, you know why. Why won't you ever tell me? What is it that I musn't know?

SON: You may know it now.

FATHER: (*To* SON) It's your fault, is it, eh? —He declined to marry into this kind of family?

SON: No, it is not my fault.

FATHER: What then? ...Why then?

SON: (*Remains silent—then*) I...don't know.

FATHER: (*Contemptuously*) Faugh!

SON: All right, there's nothing for it. It is my fault, Lisa, because—because—I am an outcast, a...

(SON *falls silent in fear, because* FATHER *desperately bursts into sobs.*)

FATHER: Don't say that. I can—I cannot hear it. My poor, poor boy...! (*Sobbing*) I love, I love you so much, but I don't know...I don't know anything... I don't understand anything. I am—I don't have the words, no words. (*Falls silent*) No one here cares about me, and you, even you, want to leave me behind. You've made your choice, you say, now you have made your choice. But that is not true; for a long time I've felt that in own house, my wife and my children. —You'd be glad if I didn't exist—I'm well aware of that.

(MOTHER *tries to intercede.*)

FATHER: Oh no, oh no, I don't need your pity. Just let me... Let me just say one thing. I have bottled it up too long. I know very well that I don't understand you, but I cannot and I feel... so alone. I am afraid that you will leave me behind. You may think it childish of me to burst into tears—but I am, I am too afraid that you will go away. I didn't mean to react so badly. I want to approve of everything. What do I care about other people! ...But now, now you're surely thinking: what an idiot...

DAUGHTER: (*Kissing him*) Father!

FATHER: (*Weakly*) Dear girl. —You are upset now too, eh. But you'll get over it, won't you, my little girl. You must put it behind you. You just forget about that loser.

(DAUGHTER, *hurt, pulls away.*)

FATHER: You are much too good for him... (*To* MOTHER) I...whatever you think is best, so do I... (*Hesitantly*) ...if it doesn't matter to you that everyone, anyway, you must know yourself— Just let me get a grip on myself. I have to collect my thoughts. I can't make sense of it all at once. I have to get a breath of fresh air (*To* DAUGHTER) Do a good deed and take a walk with your father.

SON: (*Seizes* FATHER*'s hand and squeezes it between his hands*) Father!

(DAUGHTER *and* FATHER *leave together.*)

MOTHER: (*Sighing*) Well, there, you see...

SON: (*Slowly*) Yes, Mother, it is my fault.

MOTHER: Mine too. —I simply cannot judge. I'm full of doubts, Walt. —I don't know what is good and what is bad... Oh my child... (*Falls silent*) I have wanted to serve two totally different people...both with equal love and both with pity...I would like to be everything to you and at the same time I need to be with your father too—not just out of duty, Walt, but because I love him and feel so sorry for him and because I know that I can keep him on an even keel.

SON: I understand only too well, Mother, how you've had to do double duty.

MOTHER: You won't judge your father too harshly now, will you, Walt?

SON: Oh no— (*Pause*) —Mother... (*Holds out his hand*)

MOTHER: (*Putting hers in it*) Yes, dear...

SON: (*Gentle, but emphatically*) I'm going away. —No, quiet—listen, mother. It is better if I go. Just now, with Father sitting here, I felt it strongly. —I stand between the two of you. —Ah, mother dearest! (*He weeps.*)..

MOTHER: (*Kindly*) Oh, dear, no...

SON: I think that's why I...felt hatred for him. Ah, don't deny it, Mother—

(MOTHER *lays her head on the table, weeping.*)

SON: It would have torn you apart in the long run and—then you wouldn't be able to help us.

MOTHER: (*Terrified*) Oh no, Walt.

SON: (*Comes and stands by her*) Father will not be able to bear the shame, and I—I cannot go on pretending. So let me go.

MOTHER: Alone...

SON: With my thoughts full of you, Mother.

MOTHER: No, Walt, I—I cannot be without you—

SON: Father needs you. You must stay with him. I understand that too, Mother. That is your duty. —He cannot do without you. I am young and strong. —You know what you have been to me. I shall treasure that in my heart my whole life long. I shall think of it wherever I am or whenever things go hard with me. You can do something for me now, Mother—let me go.

MOTHER: Where?

SON: I don't know that yet. But in any case far away. —Somewhere where I can be free, where no one knows me—where I...

(*As* SON *sees anxiety in* MOTHER*'s eyes*)

SON: You have to be unafraid. I shall be strong—I always have you.

MOTHER: (*Embracing him*) My dearest boy! (*Pause*) I... I must not stop you.

(MOTHER, *weeping, falls on to her chair.* SON *takes her head in his hands, kisses her hair.*)

SON: (*Gently*) Mother! ...Thank you!

(MOTHER *clasps his hands tightly in desperation, then lets him go.* —SON *exits quietly.*)

MOTHER: (*Alone*) Has it all been for nothing then?

(Curtain)

END OF PLAY

www.ingramcontent.com/pod-product-compliance
Ingram Content Group UK Ltd.
Pitfield, Milton Keynes, MK11 3LW, UK
UKHW020136250726
13967UKWH00002B/690

9 780881 454215